THE ULTIMATE GUIDE TO
MOUNTAIN BIKING
STEVE GEALL & ROBIN KITCHIN

D1573320

THE ULTIMATE GUIDE TO
MOUNTAIN BIKING

STEVE GEALL & ROBIN KITCHIN

THE LYONS PRESS

First Lyons Press edition, 2001

First published in the UK 2001
by CollinsWillow
an imprint of HarperCollins*Publishers*
London

Copyright © 2001 by HarperCollins*Publishers*

This book was created by Chilli for HarperCollins*Publishers* Ltd.

1 3 5 7 9 8 6 4 2

ISBN 1-58574-303-8

Color reproduction by Saxon Group

Printed and bound in Italy by Rotolito, Lombarda

The Library of Congress Cataloging-in-Publication Data is available on file.

Edited by: Bex Hopkins. Design by: Chilli/Dakini Ltd.
Photography: Steve Bardens

contents

1
welcome to
mountain biking

For many, mountain biking is about exploring areas of wilderness and mountains without the tedious speed (or rather lack of it) associated with walking. It's also a hell of a lot more exciting too. Every weekend, hundreds – no, *tens of thousands* of like-minded people get out on their bikes and ride, whether it be for training, fun, fresh air or to keep fit, man and bike become one and go riding. Wasteland, hills and woods all offer the mountain biker a place to ride and explore without the hassle of cars and lorries... and quite often, other people too.

It's about getting somewhere under your own steam, however fast or slow and with as many drink-stops or picnics as you fancy. Rarely done as an individual pastime, it's a gregarious sport making a long ride a social occasion as well as a day away from boring chores and commitments.

Left: "My favourite place to ride is at Buckland on the South Coast. I've built a lot of jumps there." – Steve

"if only it were all a never ending **single-track "**

For those who desire real challenge and adventure, the mountains offer the best in exciting and sometimes dangerous terrain, but where's the fun in playing it safe anyway? Being so far away from a town or city is what drives so many mountain bikers to push themselves in such difficult terrain and conditions, for those few hours or days nothing else really matters. It's just the mountains and you. No deadlines, no bills to pay, no DIY and to hell with work. The only things worth worrying about are how fast or long a descent is, how to get there and whether you've got the right tyres on for the job. It's a constant battle against terrain and gravity to reach the summit, but not only is the view and self-fulfilment worth the energy, pain and sweat induced by climbing – there's the breezy downhill to look forward to as well.

Riding for Team Animal Orange, an international mountain bike race team, means we get to ride in beautiful places all over the world. From mountains in Slovenia to the deserts of Southern California, we get to race on the toughest tracks and courses the World Circuit has to offer. Asides from our love of downhill racing we freeride across unmarked terrain and mountains to satisfy our passion for the unknown, using our race skills to descend from mountain passes taking in breathtaking scenery and cultural heavens on the way. Don't restrict yourself to the hills close to your backyard, get your bike in a box and go ride somewhere new and sunny. Hawaii, Greece, South Africa or Australia... wherever takes your fancy. Choose a travel company or simply grab a map and a couple of mates and get on that plane. We guarantee you won't be disappointed. New food, cultures and trails to ride all day long, what's stopping you?

" mountains offer the best terrain, so what are you waiting for?"

If you've been bothered to go somewhere and ride, don't let your skills be the limiting factor. There's nothing more frustrating than riding somewhere beautiful and not being able to stay on your bike. Ten miles up a mountain track isn't the ideal place to be taking a tumble or learning new techniques. That's what your local trails are for, and your mates come in pretty useful for that drive to the emergency unit if it goes really wrong.

But seriously, by improving your riding skills you'll be able to ride faster, better and more safely on harder and more extreme trails without worrying about walking sections or losing any skin. That's the plan anyway.

The best advice for enjoying your bike more is to use it as much as you can and to continually advance and learn, both technically and spiritually. So read on, then get out on those trails and make the most of the dirt beneath your wheels.

Left: It's an unbeatable feeling when you're riding on foreign soil. In this case Nidri, Lefkas, Greece.

Opposite Top: "One of the best reasons for riding is to visit new places and meet like-minded people." – Robin

"**mountain biking** has taken over **my life**"

2
where the
sport is today

The semi-official history of mountain biking (often written in a counter-cultural haze and sodden in bitchiness) is that, sometime in the mid-seventies, a disparate group of individuals in Marin County, California, looked at their vintage Schwinn Exclesior 'clunkers' and thought to themselves "I could ride down some fire trails on that". And behold! Mountain biking was born. Well, maybe... but around the same time some friends and I were taking our Raleigh Grifters, stripping all the plastic off them and... riding down some fire trails on them. So, I guess that we were the pioneers of mountain biking as well.

The point I'm trying to make is that people have been riding bikes off-road for a long, long time, but the difference is that the Californians took the idea further and started adapting – and eventually building – bikes for the purpose.

Originally, mountain biking was purely downhilling. There was little thought of riding the bikes up the hills – that's what pick-ups are for. The bikes were too heavy,

under-geared and, frankly, where was the fun in it anyway? So downhilling was where it was at, and that's how it stayed for a long time. The main performance-enhancing modifications that the Marin pioneers made to their poor old fat-tyred clunkers were strengthening the frame (so that it stayed together for at least a couple of runs) and improving the brakes, for more efficient stopping at the bottom. As it happened, Marin County was – and still is – one of the main centres of US road racing. The roadies were considerably fitter than the mountain bikers, but in the eyes of many, riding the asphalt was seriously lacking in fun and mountain biking soon attracted many riders more used to skinny road tyres. These new roadie converts to the ways of the fat tyre wanted to use their fitness to ride bikes up the hill as well as down – bringing with them the idea of 'earning' the fun part (going downhill), something which is integral in many outdoor and mountain pursuits.

Top Left: "Sometimes I just need to take a break and enjoy the beautiful places I get to ride." – Robin

Left: A sunny day for a huge drop into a disused quarry – Doncaster, Yorkshire, England.

Right: Trials riding is a dynamic growth area – have a go at finding the balance point on the ground first.

With this new influence, bikes and components started to be specially built. Rather than using an old clunker frame, people like Tom Ritchey (then producing frames for Charlie Kelly and Gary Fisher's Mountain Bike company) and Joe Breeze used their frame-building skills from building road bikes to create specific mountain bike frames, which were both lighter and stronger than the adapted clunkers. Noting the popularity of this trend, Mike Sinyard of Specialized Bicycles, then an importer of European components into the US, studied the mountain bikes produced by the likes of Fisher and Breeze and created the original Specialized Stumpjumper, the first mass-produced mountain bike made in Japan. At its first airing at the Long Beach Bicycle Show in 1982, the 'Stumpy' became a hit, selling 500 units in its first two weeks. The MTB boom had begun.

At the same time, plenty of thought was going into componentry. The original back-pedal coaster brakes found on the clunkers were superseded by cyclo-cross cantilever brakes, which were lighter and far more powerful. Various gear systems were used and abused, and thumb-shifters became the choice for changing the increasing number of gears. Companies such as Wilderness Trail Bikes and Sun Tour developed many interesting and often ridiculous components. However, all of this was fairly moot when a large Japanese manufacturer of fishing reels decided they had to diversify, and that cycling was where they were going to go. The original Shimano Deore 'groupset' was the first integrated set of mass-market components specifically designed for mountain biking, and realistically opened the door for the mass-production of affordable mountain bikes.

Opposite: The latest full suspension
bike from the Orange bike range.

Right: "Before suspension bikes came along some areas
were unrideable." Verdon, Provence, France. – Robin

Moving into the late eighties, the path of mountain biking was aiming firmly in a cross-country direction. The aim was to have a bike that was good at climbing and downhilling, and similarly riders were developing fitness and skills to accomplish both. The first official Mountain Bike World Championships – held in Durango, Colorado, – in 1990 included categories for hill-climb, cross-country (XC) and downhill (DH), the overall winner chosen by having the highest score in all of these disciplines.

It wasn't until the late eighties that specialisation started creeping back into the sport. The introduction of the first usable suspension forks, the RockShox RS1 and the Manitou, split riders down the middle. The purist cross-country riders derided the forks for their 'hefty' weight, supposed unreliability, and for what they considered the reduction in riding skill required when using them. Others, probably truer to mountain biking's downhilling roots, realised that new technology could be used to increase speed. It was at this point that the downhill/cross-country split in the sport started.

"who cares what type of riding you do as long as you enjoy it"

During the nineties, downhilling and cross-country specialised to such a degree that it was virtually impossible for one person to excel in both disciplines. Downhill courses got steeper, rougher and harder as downhill bikes developed longer and better suspension, both front and rear, to the stage we have now where a top-level downhill bike closely resembles a motocross bike without the engine. Cross-country courses became flatter and smoother, perhaps to match the influx of road racers into the sport, and the top-level riders became smaller and skinnier as power-to-weight ratio became what decided races. Relative skill levels changed dramatically, a World Cup cross-country course could be ridden by anyone on a Sunday ride whereas a World Cup downhill course could only just be walked down. Levels of fitness in cross-country shot up, as did levels of drunkenness in downhill!

Around the late nineties, downhillers remembered that they were athletes as well as drunkards and started training for fitness again. With better technology, downhill bikes have become lighter as well as stronger, as winning margins became as tight as hundredths of a second. In cross-country, whilst the bikes are more about refinement than technological leaps, the same cannot be said about the riders' bodies. The level of fitness now required is as great or greater than any sport, and was reflected in cross-country's introduction to the Olympics in the 1996 Atlanta Games. France has become the real powerhouse in mountain bike sport, with World Champions in cross-country and downhill, and a governing body that eagerly supports the development of young riders.

Away from racing, the emergence of a hardcore jumping subculture, crossing over with BMX, motocross and snowboarding, has been the main new movement in the sport. Reflected in the popularity of one-on-one dual racing, this is probably the most spectacular and exciting development in the sport for years, and is a real grass-roots movement harking back to those early Marin days. Cheap (the bike are basic 'hardtails' – that is, without rear suspension), democratic (find some quiet wasteland and build your own trails) and visually spectacular, most young riders now think of themselves as dirt jumpers. At the same time, the variety of events in biking has diversified, from the Megavalanche races in the French and Swiss Alps (mass start, 20-mile downhill races) to team endurance events such as the Twenty Four Hours of Moab and Canaan, to the Polaris multi-day wilderness events. Although these are all competitive events, they encourage the participation by anyone for the sheer sake and glory of simply having taken part and survived.

That is precisely one of the main attractions of mountain biking. You don't have to do it, you do it for the hell of it, and you get the choice of how you want to do it. And that, really, is the point.

Opposite: Riding in the winter blows away the cobwebs and maintains your fitness level. North Yorkshire, England.

Above: Bird's eye view of the many scenic tracks on Lefkas, Greece.

Right: Trials is just one of the ways you can defeat gravity with your bike.

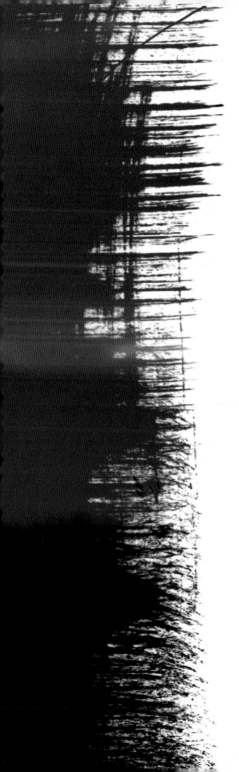

3

getting started

Attitude is all you need to get started in mountain biking. Well, okay, a bike helps too, but you've got to want to do it. No mountain biker ever became any good by accident. Having the right attitude is essential, but it needn't be the 'good' attitude that they taught you at school, just a desire to test yourself against the terrain with a bike, which you'll become too attached to, in a strange, emotional way. Don't try to resist – you will love your bike, so be proud of it and treat it like it should be! Hard, bad and always fast, never ride within your limits as you'll only be dissatisfied.

Back to the bike. I started on a friend's bike. I would strongly recommend it, especially if the bike in question is too big and slightly out of date. Then go riding with your friends who, of course, will be more experienced than you are. If you happen to be borrowing one of their bikes, show them you can – and will – keep up. That's the attitude I mean! Next you'll want to get a decent bike, one that fits you and one with brakes that work and enough gears to show the boys you mean business.

Left: Treat each ride as a personal challenge.

If cash is tight, get the best that you can't afford. You'll only wish you'd spent more on a better bike later, as you improve. There's nothing worse than being limited by your equipment. Just make sure you get a bike that fits properly and has a good quality frame, the rest can be changed or up-graded at a later date as the parts wear out.

A lot of mountain bikers came to the sport via other 'freesports' such as motocross and BMX, snowboarding and skiing. They all require the same degree of passion and love of speed and danger. It also helps if you like getting muddy and spending time in the great outdoors.

how we started

"I've always done sports, mainly windsurfing which hasn't really helped me with any part of my riding in particular. I'm not a gracious rider but I take risks and more often than not I pull it off. My riding is almost the opposite to Steve Geall's, he's a much more calculated rider than me. I've always hurt myself whatever I'm doing, so it seems natural to hurt myself on my bike. Thankfully, it's never seemed to affect me mentally. Being part of an international team and getting the chance to ride all over the world means that when I am injured I miss out on riding cool places. So I get back on my bike as soon as possible.

Before university I spent most of my life on the beach, hanging out, windsurfing and partying. Most of my mates started riding and racing mountain bikes so I had a go and seemed to be going as fast as most of them. A bit more out of control maybe, but just as fast. From then on I've been racing and, over the years, it's gradually taken over my life. I've become more relaxed and less competitive and in a way it's helped me ride more smoothly and faster. But mainly my success has been due to being part of such a strong and close-knit team."
– Robin

"I started riding mountain bikes because I achieved my goals in BMX. I was World Ramp Champion in 1988 and couldn't really get any better than that. It was a natural progression as all my mates rode mountain bikes. I started racing MTBs in 1994 with the Animal team and started to do really well. In 1996 I rode in the Pro-Elite category and started racing in World Cup races, I still race a lot and ride BMX, I do a lot of promotional riding too. My advice for anyone about to start racing is to ride your bike as much as you can and learn from your mistakes. Always work on your weaknesses and never keep going back to what you're good at, keep learning and practising. The more time you spend on the bike, the more relaxed you'll be, so if it goes wrong you'll stay more relaxed and remember never just grab for the brakes or tense up. Most importantly, learn about what you want from your bike and how it works, spend time setting the suspension up properly and making it work best for you." – **Steve**

33

staying fluid ⁴

Knowing what to do is only the start of riding better, combining it with timing is how to make it work properly. Timing is about predicting what's coming next and dealing with it by putting together several actions in the right order and at the right time.

I remember the times (and there are many of them) that I have used too much front brake and somehow ended up swallowing more than a fair portion of dust and gravel. It wasn't the fault of braking too hard on the front that caused the crash, more a product of hitting a rock or root at the wrong time whilst braking. An obvious example perhaps, but a good case study that making the bike do exactly what you want – and when you want – can help you out. It's about anticipating the worst and adapting your plan of action to suit the terrain.

More importantly, staying 'at one' with your bike allows you to get away with more moments of indecision or slightly wrong timing. Think about the time you pulled off a jump when you were riding along a new trail, simply because it all looked safe and easy and you didn't notice the lip of a small jump. Next thing you know, you're back on the ground and somehow you landed it. No anticipation, no nerves, no problem, meaning you were totally relaxed and balanced.

Think of your bike as a tool to allow your body to progress along a trail as smoothly as possible. If you watch a downhiller race, he will push and pull the bike all over the place whilst his body will take the fastest and shortest line. He makes the bike do most of the work and keeps his head focused on what's coming next.

Staying fluid is about keeping momentum going and using speed to overcome obstacles. Think about the time you hit a bumpy patch of ground a bit faster than you'd normally be comfortable with. If your weight was well-balanced over the bike and you weren't on the brakes, then you probably got away with it. In fact, you probably rode it better and more smoothly than ever before. Unless forced to do otherwise, your bike will follow the contours of the land. With added speed, the bike will skim over the bumps instead of going up and down over each one. By gliding or skimming over them, the bike would have responded less to the contours and if aided by you, staying flexible and relaxed on the bike, together you would have flowed over the obstacle better.

Being fluid depends on how your body reacts to the bike and the contours of the ground. Try relaxing and bending your elbows and knees more; use them like shock absorbers. If the bike does something unexpected and your limbs are bent, then you lessen the chance of a jerky reaction. Instead, your limbs will take up the slack and respond in a more controlled manner, lessening the chance of over-reacting.

I can't think how many times I have narrowly missed a tree or lamp post only to have swerved into something else, in my case usually something more expensive or sharp than the original obstacle! Funny afterwards (when the cuts have healed) but so easily avoided with a controlled reaction instead of panic.

Putting together a number of techniques in a short space of time takes practice but it does come and is amazingly difficult to lose once learnt. Staying fluid and good timing are essential in any sport, whether it is rally driving, football or any form of cycling. It's a hard thing to describe but when you've got it, you won't ever look back. Except to see how far your riding buddies are behind you.

" looking ahead is the key to keeping it smooth "

5

going uphill

There's something strangely rewarding about riding uphill. It's not natural, but it is a means to an end. Basically, it means you get to the top of the hill, which means lots of fun coming back down again.

To the more serious cross-country racers, a climb is the perfect place to make a move on the opposition, the strongest in mind and body will be the first to ascend causing a major psychological barrier between himself and the officially 'dropped' riders. Apparently there's some sort of satisfaction in seeing other people hurting up a climb and then in some bizarre mind-over-matter way punishing themselves more just to make a point of being the first to the top. I never really saw the point, but that's why I'm the best bike pusher there is. Sometimes climbs just feel better to walk and leaves me with more energy to spend on the way down.

You've got to give it to the cross-country riders though; they do manage to climb up some technical and challenging tracks. These bits require much thought and skill and there's no time to worry about the burning calf muscles here. Approaching a rock ledge at barely five miles an hour gives you enough time to consider jumping off and running (nah, that looks pathetic) or pulling a wheelie. That sounds painful, especially as you'll then have to hop the rear end over the ledge too. Fit that in around a lot of pedalling and you've got some serious effort, skill and endurance requirements.

Timing is everything on a technical climb. Balance and skill feature strongly but if you can't put them in the right order at the right time, you'll be walking to the top.

Choosing a smooth line is one of the best ways to succeed, look for areas of solid ground, you don't want to be losing traction if it's steep. Keep your weight well

back over the rear wheel and don't put too much power down at any one time. Think smooth and calculated and try to keep momentum going without stopping and starting pedalling. Choose a low gear to allow for easy pedalling but one that's high enough to make some decent progress, twiddling up a climb looks pretty dumb and wastes lots of energy too. 'Do I stand or sit?' is a question often asked about climbing technique, and there's no real right or wrong answer. It all depends on how you feel and what the terrain is like – most importantly, the gradient and how loose the surface is. If it's hard and steep then try to power up the climb, attacking out of the saddle to minimise the amount of time spent on the slope and keeping momentum flowing.

If it's more technical, ie rocky with loose sand or gravel, then pick your line to include more solid-looking sections and avoid the loose bits, they only sap your speed and energy and slow you down.

On really steep climbs, take care not to let the front wheel rise too far, especially when you are sitting down. Use the nose of the saddle to sit on to ensure enough traction over the rear wheel whilst keeping the front end in control and on the ground. It's all too easy to let the front end wobble around as you haul on the bars. This will upset your rhythm and timing and cause you to zig-zag your way to the top. And let's face it, you really don't want to spend any more time on a gruelling climb than you really have to.

Opposite: Stretch your legs and spend some time out of the saddle.

Below: Keep your weight well centred over the wheels and a smooth pedalling rhythm.

riders' tips

"Experiment with using the saddle to distribute your weight differently, that way you'll be able to put the right amount of traction on whichever wheel you need to at exactly the right time. Also, work on holding your body weight over the bars whilst standing up. This gives your legs a breather for a while. On really long climbs that are technically unchallenging, try standing up and pedalling for twenty revolutions and then sitting for twenty, that way you'll maintain your rhythm and mentally be better able to deal with the pain better.

Remember to breathe, try pushing the air out of your lungs to prevent a 'stitch' or cramps, you'll find your lungs will automatically take in fresh air again. It sounds and looks better than taking in big gulps, a good way to make out you're not as tired or strained as your opposition. A mental win, if nothing else!

Getting into a rhythm and breathing properly is a technique I use when out training. I can then block out any unwanted thoughts and deal with the task in hand – beating the hill and reaching that awesome view at the top." – **Robin**

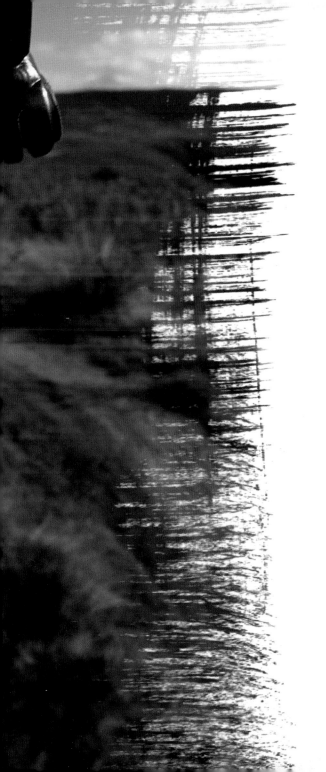

slowing down ⁶

Braking

You probably know all about braking: you pull the levers as hard as you can and the bike slows down. Simple. Well, yes... and no, not really. Although braking *is* slowing down, effective use of the brakes can actually help you keep a higher speed through a corner. This is how it works: effective use of the brakes is when you keep as much speed as possible through a corner (if the trail was straight, you wouldn't be slowing down, would you?). Keep this in mind – slow the bike by just the right amount at just the right time.

The first thing to know about braking is the brakes themselves. The history of mountain bikes is pretty much the story of brakes. The early mountain bikers of Marin County, being entirely concerned with riding fire trails at top speed and growing ridiculous facial hair, didn't care much for brakes or indeed slowing down at all and, bearing in mind what they had to use, that's probably just as well. The first 'clunkers' were fitted with rear coaster brakes. These tended to burn out after one or two runs – the infamous Repack Races

of 1976–1981 were named after the fact that the hubs needed re-packing with grease after each run. This was due to the heat produced by a hugely stressed coaster brake doing what it was never intended to. Once riders started riding uphill they needed something lighter, and they fitted Mafac cantilever brakes. Mountain bikes stayed with the basic cantilever until the mid-nineties, when Shimano was the first to mass-produce the long-arm cantilever, side-pull or 'V' brake. First seen in public on French multi-World Champion Nicolas Vouilloz's downhill GT bike, these caused something of a sensation and are still the standard MTB brake. In an ironic display of what comes around goes around, downhillers decided that they needed something more powerful and moved back to hub-mounted brakes, be they disc or experimental internal hub brake designs. Only these days they don't need quite so much attention or maintenance.

Opposite: Make full use of your braking potential and with disc brakes – the power is amazing.

Right: In extremely muddy conditions disc brakes are the only brake that can guarantee total stopping power.

'Feel' the brakes

The most important set-up factor about your brakes – more important than sheer power – is 'feel' or 'modulation'. What we mean by this is that the feel of the brakes at the lever should be predictable and reliable in relation to the brakes' power. Ideally, the brake would be linear, meaning that each and every pull on the lever would give you a consistent and controllable amount of braking force. Instant pitching over the handlebar (stick-in-the-spokes-style) or a lever that you pull to the bars with nothing happening (the 'oh my God, a deep hole, approaching rapidly, damn that hurts' school of brakes) kind of says your brakes aren't quite right. Disc brakes are the best in this respect, but V-brakes hold their own until the speed gets silly or it gets wet. How the lever feels when applying the brakes is a matter of personal preference. Some like the lever to do nothing, then to come on hard; other riders like the brakes to be working the second you look at the lever. Only you can decide what you like best, so experiment on a trail that you know well.

To get back to the act of braking itself, what are we trying to achieve? Well, we want to slow the bike just enough that we can get round an obstacle at the maximum possible speed. What we don't want to be doing is hurtling into a corner at mach speed and, finding out that we have no traction, heading straight for a very solid-looking tree. Believe me, you will come off worse. Collar bone versus large oak tree? No contest. At the same time, crawling around a corner makes you look like a big girl's blouse and your friends will point and laugh.

So: slow the bike when *approaching* the corner. Brake as late as you feel safe, using plenty of lever, and only slow down as much as you need to. This may sound obvious but it is a common problem to over-brake, everybody does it. The idea, after all, is to maintain the highest average speed. What you have to develop is the experience to judge what the bike is doing, what speed you will be able to get round the corner at, and how you will be able to carry maximum speed through the corner. What you don't want to be doing is braking too hard, finding yourself too slow and having to pedal hard to get back up to speed. Judging the difference between the two is the knack.

Opposite: Perfect terrain for practising braking – dirt tracks near Nidri, Lefkas, Greece.

Weighting

Once again, body position and weighting of the bike is everything. Braking is more efficient when the body and bike are working together, resulting in slowing down more efficiently and in control. If the terrain is loose, then it is best to have your centre of gravity over the centre of the bike and as low as possible, to correct any rapid or random movements the bike may make in a response to braking. Going from solid to loose or slippery ground, braking and cornering usually causes the wheels to lose traction and as a result you only try to brake harder, which can open up a big can of pain. Once traction is gone you don't get it back by thinking "what I really need to do now is brake some more". An alteration to body position or weighting of the bike can pitch you off without the slightest bit of notice. If you're not sure of the terrain, stay well-centred with equal amounts of weight on the front and rear wheels.

A useful point to remember is that under normal straight and flat conditions, your weight on the bike is distributed pretty much evenly, maybe slightly more on the rear but there's not much difference. Acceleration causes weight to be transferred to the rear wheel, and braking

Opposite: The set-up of your brakes is crucial to reliable braking.

Below: "Controlling the rear wheel as it drifts wide comes with practice." – Robin

puts more weight to the front of the bike. This means that more is done by the front brake, as that's where the traction is under braking, thus its role in slowing down is more important. However, a quick snatch of the front brake lever leads to more crashes than a harsh pull of the rear lever (the aforementioned stick-in-the-spokes syndrome – usually painful and often embarrassing). Using more front brake needs to be learned, practised and judged well, and the set-up of the brakes is fundamental to controlled and reliable braking.

Position of both the bike and rider becomes more vital the steeper the slope or the greater deceleration required. On steep sections, the bike will carry more speed due to the effects of gravity, pushing your weight backwards over the rear wheel. Steep descents require body weight to be further over the rear wheel – the steeper the gradient, the more weight is required to be over the back wheel. This allows the rear wheel more traction when braking, so helping to slow the bike down as much as possible. It also prevents you being pitched over the bars at high speed and probably

landing right on your head, with the bike landing on top, just to add insult to injury. Braking on the front wheel should be kept to a minimum. If you are unsure or if it's really steep, any loss of traction or the front wheel locking-up can cause the bike to pitch forwards or sideways allowing gravity to take its toll. Braking on the rear is always safer on downhills and can often be used to help corner. A well-timed and controlled snatch of the brake lever can allow the rear wheel to drift wide, encouraging the bike to turn-in. Working in conjunction with weighting the outside of the bike, braking can lead to rapid changes in direction.

On steep gradients or muddy conditions it's usually best to feather the brakes and to avoid pulling harshly at the levers. Try gently pulling on the levers until the bike almost skids and then letting go again. It is a way of scrubbing-off speed without continually braking, allowing you to maintain control and steering.

" the better you are at braking, the faster you can ride "

Testing it out

Choose your favourite trail or singletrack section, something that has plenty of corners, nothing too nasty but challenging and fun, and ride it several times, choosing different lines and braking at different points along the way. If you're really serious about improving and understanding how and when to brake, then try timing yourself through the section. Nothing too accurate or technical, but a simple stopwatch or clock should be enough to show any improvements. This is how the best downhillers learn and improve on technical sections. It helps

them choose the fastest lines for race day – if it works for them, then it could work for you. Often following a better or faster rider through a section helps. They may brake later or earlier than you feel safe doing and by trying to stay with them you can break any patterns or problems you may have, whether you realised you had them or not.

There is also the competitive factor too, no-one likes being beaten, and by following another rider any fear can be reduced. If you do crash because of late braking or not making the corner, have

another go and brake a touch earlier or choose a line you are more confident with until you fancy pushing the limits again. More often than not, it's at this point that the maximum speed or latest braking point has been found, and it might be an idea to back-off for a while as over-practice or trying too hard can be counter-productive. A good way to keep within your learning limit is to play or practice until you get tired or don't feel you're learning any more. At this point, go and do something else or ride another section, it's all about not getting stale and more importantly having that feeling of achievement that comes with improving and learning. Plus, riding over one of your mates when they stack it is always good for a laugh.

Above all, remember that better braking will make you a faster rider overall. It is easier and more fun to learn than putting in hours of sprint training just to make up a few extra seconds.

Opposite: Who said skidding isn't fun?

Right: Enjoy using your brakes – sparingly?

7
cornering

"races are often won or lost on corners"

It might seem pretty obvious, but if you're riding in a straight line then you can pretty much ride at whatever speed you feel like. By contrast, corners have an optimum speed at which traction and momentum work in harmony with the rider and bike, allowing a smooth change of direction.

All corners are different – the angle, radius, gradient, surface and terrain all pose different problems and each must be analysed and tackled in a specific way. You can roughly categorise corner types into the following groups:
• Bermed corners – where a corner has a defined or raised bank as an outer limit or perimeter

- Off-camber corners – where the ground drops away from the direction you want to go
- Decreasing radius corners – the corner tightens along its length
- Increasing radius corners – the corner opens up along its length

Corners form the most important areas of a track or course. Most other obstacles can be avoided or ridden around but if you need to change direction quickly – and it happens to the best of us – then you have to corner. The importance of cornering properly cannot be emphasised enough; races are usually won or lost in corners. Dual racing is a great example: two riders on a course packed with jumps and corners, the first rider around the first corner more often than not takes the race. If not, then you can guarantee they were taken on a corner.

Away from racing, the best place to leave your riding buddies behind in the dust is through corners.

Left & Right: Sometimes you just have to trust your tyres.

Bermed corners

Bermed corners are defined by a positive camber, be it man-made or a natural bank. On race courses, berms are used to help keep the flow or momentum around corners, enabling racers to concentrate on the more technical parts of the course.

To keep your speed up, try to enter the berm wide and high following the highest contour possible. Use all of the available bank to ensure max speed around the berm and, most importantly, on the way out of it.

riders' tips

"If you think of the banking as preventing the wheels from sliding out wide, you can push the bike against the berm and create a greater exit speed – think centrifugal force. Shifting your body weight to the outside of the bike helps with this technique.

The steepness of the berm naturally allows for plenty of pedal clearance, which is exaggerated by leaning over, so there's no need to worry about catching a pedal on the ground. Once you feel comfortable not pulling those chicken sticks in a berm then try putting in a few pedal strokes. You'll be amazed how fast you actually can go without losing any flesh. Leaning over also allows your tyres to gain maximum grip, so you can ride tighter turns faster than you have ever dared before. Just keep pedalling as long as possible and prepare to enter a new dimension on the exit."
– **Robin**

Opposite: "The sheer feeling of speed and power railing round a berm is a hard one to beat." – Robin

Off-camber

The complete opposite of a bermed corner is the truly rancid off-camber corner. They look wrong, feel wrong and generally are a pain in the ass because gravity is working against you and the bike. They are typified by having to turn across sloping ground *against* the angle of slope.

Both slope and the nature of cornering pulls the bike towards the outside of the corner. Off-camber corners also tend to defeat riders in psychological terms too, try not to look at the lower edges of the corner and focus on the apex or higher ground.

As the slope increases, there is more chance of grounding a pedal and getting pitched off into the bushes. Attack the corner and maintain enough speed into the bend to keep momentum through the corner. Keep off those brakes as much as possible and weight the wheels evenly to add traction. Don't lean, and keep your weight in the middle of the bike and as close to the centre of gravity as possible.

I reckon it is best to spend as little time in off-camber sections as possible, it's the only way of reducing the risk of stacking. You never get any prior warning with these types of corners, one minute it all seems fine and dandy and then your wheels have slipped sideways and gone AWOL.

Above: "It's so satisfying getting a corner right, even if it takes a few attempts."

Below: "When the terrain is so bumpy and steep it's easy for the front wheel to get caught up on something and if you're touching the front brake, it's game over!"
— Robin

riders' tips

"There are a few ways to tackle an off-camber corner, but as with all technical things, they take a bit of practice and rely on perfect timing and balance to perfect. You could 'square off' the turn. This is where you keep as straight and upright for as long as possible then abruptly change direction, in effect attacking the slope. Depending on the surface, you may be able to use a little rear brake to help skid the rear around the turn. You'll have to pull the front wheel up and over any obstacles, to help haul the bike round the corner. This technique gives you a high exit line, which (if you're clever enough) you can use to your advantage in a race situation. Anyway, it prevents you ending up in the ditch near the exit, if nothing else.

In shorter corners try turning sharply before the off-camber and stay vertical over the camber change or apex. In other words, make the steering change after or before the most drastic off-camber part.

Obvious tips are keep your pedals in a horizontal position as much as possible and keep braking to a minimum. Actually, it's best not to brake at all, as it will only load the front wheel and cause it to slide out.

Along with the braking thing, avoid weight transfers in off-camber corners. Set it up right first and stay nearly vertical if possible. If you feel a tad sketchy then keep your inside foot off the pedal and ready to dab the ground if needed." – **Robin**

Flat turns

Generally, flat turns are the easiest kind of turn to learn. Even just riding along the road to work, school or the corner shop involves flat turns, so you'd imagine there's not much to learn here. But it's your line choice that is of most importance. Usually the tightest line through the apex is the fastest, mainly because it's the shortest. Hitting that line depends on the surface and terrain; if it's rocky or rooty, you may have to compromise the tightest line for a faster and smoother choice.

Open and flat turns allow more time for preparation, you'll have enough time to choose a point at which to turn and even have a chance to locate an exit point. Leaning the bike and body towards the inside of the corner aids turning and puts more weight over the outside of the bike, especially if your outer pedal is lower. This forces the bike around the turn, meaning that you have less steering to worry about and more energy and attention to choose a line and pedal out of the corner. If the terrain is open and smooth, you may as well lean over from the beginning, especially if you're going fast. That way you'll stay fluid and smooth, maintaining traction between tyres and terra firma.

A more advanced technique is to put more body weight on the front wheel. Loading the front end makes the bike stay on line in open corners. Nervous riders tend to keep more body weight back over the rear end – in corners, try to be more positive and attack the corner, this will help you load the front more and in turn go faster and become more confident. A positive 'catch-22' situation, if you like.

Use 'easy' corners like these to your advantage. You'll have the time to set the corner up and the speed to stick to your line, so make the bike go where you want. If that means pushing other riders wide, then use it to your own ends. Get those elbows ready and nudge your way through the pack.

Left: "Setting up a corner correctly is crucial."
– Robin

Opposite: Dual descender racing – you'll see plenty of elbow action in the corners.

riders' tips

"Look for rocks or small mounds to act as mini-berms, these help keep your wheels in the turn and are a good reference point to aim for to initiate the turn.

If you are racing, take the tighter line and push opponents wide. The inside line always has the upper hand, make the most of it.

Be committed to the maximum speed that you feel safe with, and lean as much as feels possible. Remember, you can always lean over a little further and go that bit faster. If you don't crash, then you weren't that close to the edge. Give it another try and knock it up a gear.

If you're attacking the same corner at increasing speeds, try to stay on the tighter line, that way you can always let the bike run wide if you start to feel unstable or it goes pear-shaped. Running wide on the exit can help to maintain speed at the crucial stage, allowing you to accelerate away faster." – **Robin**

Decreasing radius

Riding a turn that gets tighter and sharper as it goes on (a decreasing radius) requires more steering than most turns. If it is off-camber too, then you're going to have your work cut out for you.

There are many ways of handling a decreasing radius corner. Thinking about it in terms of shape can help. Will your line reflect the shape of the corner? Or will it be completely different? You could choose an apex point and, right into the corner at high speed, brake harshly and then abruptly turn at the apex. Or double apex the turn by effectively turning twice to arrive at the exit. This is called 'squaring off the corner' by some riders. Quite literally it is treating the turn as if it were a square – entering the corner on the tight line and riding past the middle of the corner and turning on the wide line, then turning again to exit on the tight line. It takes a lot of skill and experience to judge this type of technique, but it is used by some of the best downhill racers, so it is worth a go.

For a smooth turn, going in a bit slower may allow you to start accelerating sooner, giving you the chance to make up time on the opposition.

Below: "You have to attack a corner if you want to apex it properly." – Robin

" slowing down before a turn can help you exit faster "

riders' tips

"A corner is there to force you to slow at some point; you should decide where to slow. Don't let the corner dictate your line choice too much.

Exit speed is far more important than the speed at which you enter the corner. What's the point in hitting a corner flat out if you only have to brake hard and then try to make up the lost speed in a state of panic? It only causes the bike and rider to be off-balance and potentially lose traction. It's better to go into a corner a bit slower and in control, leaving you in a better position to deal with any unexpected complications. A slightly slower entry speed means you are better balanced over the bike and able to pedal if possible, giving you the upper hand to burn off other riders on exit.

On smooth surfaces, going as wide as you can on exit feels like you've just made the corners at the fastest possible speed. But, making the most of the whole track may not be quickest line. Try a tighter line at the same speed – if it starts feeling sketchy you can always let bike go wider and be safe again." – **Robin**

Increasing radius

Sometimes on a tricky corner it pays to source the ideal exit point. Then work backwards from the exit to find out the best entry point and speed to use.

Choose a lower gear to help pedal out of the corner easier, try changing down into an easier gear as you approach the corner. That way you'll be able to pull away without causing your calf muscles to explode and you'll be prepared for any obstacles in the corner.

Keeping off the brakes unless skidding will help you make the corner by putting the rear wheel wide. Feathering the brakes going into a corner helps keep maximum traction and allows you to be centrally balanced over the bike in preparation for the turn.

The faster the entry speed, the wider the bike wants to go. Bear this in mind as you approach the corner and check out where you'll end up if it goes badly wrong. Spot the safest place to land, just in case!

Left: "Having a physical reason to turn can help even if it looks too tight." – Robin

riders' tips

"Use reference points to remind you when to initiate braking, turning etc. Don't get fixated though, you may well hit the very thing you were aiming to turn before, so keep your reference points or number of reminders to a minimum.

Mastering corners adds a new dimension to riding but the next step involves putting all those learned skills together to tackle series of corners as you'd experience them in a racing environment or on a new section of downhill trail.

Riding a series of corners well involves even more concentration and staying more fluid and balanced than ever. You also have to bear in mind all those important points about entry and exit speeds. The more corners that are linked together, the more you'll have to maintain speed to make the next turn.

Again it's not necessarily best to enter as fast as possible, you may detract from the exit speed and balance through the turn. Sacrifice some entry speed for earlier power delivery and drive on exit, it's better than backing off and having to pedal between each turn. That is a waste of energy and causes an upset in weight distribution front-to-rear leading to traction problems if the ground is loose or slippery.

Staying as flowing and smooth as possible will aid momentum through the turns and allow you put all the turns together better.

Sometimes to go slow is faster. It may feel faster to hammer into a corner, but lots of braking followed by erratic pedalling often isn't quicker.

Correct timing is the treasured key that unlocks the mystery of smooth, fast and controlled turns." – **Robin**

8

going downhill

Stay balanced, keep loose

For most mountain bikers, the ultimate reason to ride is to make the most of the downhill sections. Exploring the countryside is one thing, but there's no better feeling than screaming down a hill with the full force of gravity behind you. Feeling the pull of your bike against the brakes and battling with the urge to let them off just for the sheer hell of it – whatever the consequences.

Staying balanced and loose on the bike is essential to keeping on your chosen line. Letting the bike run or roll, allowing the bike to finds its own path, allows you to concentrate on your chosen body line. There are no rules here, as long as you and the bike flow together down the hill in some form of control you should be fine. Fighting the bike and forcing it to take an unnatural or obscure line may result in a huge stack, and there's no worse way of spoiling all that lovely momentum than using it to remove your flesh!

"don't fight the bike,
let it choose a route through
the rough stuff"

On the other hand, don't let the bike take control either. How many times have I allowed the bike to choose a line, only to be brought back down to earth a moment later? – and I mean that literally. It's a fine line between forcing the bike to take a line and letting it buck and skip beneath you whilst you continue along your chosen path. You'll know when you get it right as all those feelings of panic and fear will leave you and a feeling of harmony will replace them. With experience, learning to brake less and to stay at a higher speed will feel more natural, and if you are relaxed there is less chance of crashing or losing it.

More specifically, controlling your speed and cornering properly will allow you to gain even more satisfaction from your descent. Take on board all the lessons of cornering and braking and apply them to going downhill, only think about them a bit more carefully, as this time there is a lot more speed involved. Thinking about where and when to brake helps, remember to look much further ahead than you would riding a flat section. Quite literally, look about two bike lengths down the track and think about what is coming up next, not where or what you are riding over at that

moment in time. If you have reached the point you're thinking about, then it is already too late to make a decision on what to do. Game over! The faster you're going, the more you need to look ahead and read the track to allow yourself more time to prepare for the obstacle.

Positioning

Balance and position on the bike is even more fundamental to how the bike reacts to bumps and jumps at high speeds and on steep slopes. Too much weight forward and say goodbye to your teeth, but too much weight back and watch your front wheel slide out in the corners. Grabbing a fistful of rear brake causes the rear end to slip, slide and skid. Which is obviously fun, but doesn't mean you can predict which side of the spiky tree you'll be ending up. Remember to 'feather' (gently applying and letting off the brake to maintain a constant level of speed or control) the brakes more, especially on gravel or loose

ground. That way, your bike will respond in a controlled manner and you can apply more brake if necessary. Using the rear brake can help to make a corner at the last minute, pushing the rear wheel out wide and letting the bike turn more effectively at speed. As long as the wheel isn't locked up, braking increases traction between the tyre and the ground, so bear that in mind when you pull a load of brake on. It will change the flow of you and the bike, so anticipating this is everything to prevent a rapid change in speed, traction or orientation. Also, check out the terrain and surface before touching the brakes; avoid braking over a rocky section or on slippery roots. Rocks are better tackled faster to help you roll over them. Just pull up on the bars an amount dependent on how high they protrude from the ground. Hanging your body back over the rear wheel slightly will help you to absorb the shock of hitting rocks at speed and therefore help stabilise the bike as it slows down due to the jolts.

Opposite: Try to glide over the rocks and stay well balanced and relaxed on the bike.

Right: Hanging off the back with loose knees helps absorb the bumps.

Positioning yourself at a mid-point of balance on the bike between the two wheels is a good start and then move around in a fluid manner to where it feels most secure as the terrain changes.

It's quite easy really: you do all the same things and in the same order as you would riding on the flat, but just a bit quicker. If it's really steep, then the weight-over-the-rear-wheel trick is crucial. Practice pushing your weight back and then regaining a normal position afterwards; this transference of weight helps with traction and balance even more so when you are going faster and on steep terrain.

Keeping your knees and arms bent is much more important on technical descents. With more bumps to absorb, stay as flexible as you can on the bike.

Allow the bike to move both from side-to-side and front-to-back and transfer your weight relative to the bike moves to stay in harmony with it. A stiff body will only fight against the bike, which ultimately spells disaster. If you are scared or nervous, it is better to start slower on an easier track and work up to something bigger or faster as you improve, that way at least you'll be relaxed and stay on the bike.

Opposite: Keep your weight back and stay off the brakes.

Right: Remember to keep your arms and legs bent and go with the flow.

Rocks & boulders

If you get time to check out obstacles, such as large boulders or rocks, think about pre-jumping them. Instead of slamming into the boulder or trying to turn around it, push the bike into the ground about a length before the boulder and use the compression force to help pull the bike up and jump or bunny-hop over it. Try on smaller rocks first, even if you just get the front end over, you should skim it and keep your speed. A faster pace will help ensure more stability. Full suspension bikes let you get away with more lines and greater speed over rocky sections, with the suspension travel absorbing the bumps and shocks leaving you to think about what is coming up next. Pre-jumping allows you to take control of the course and decide where to pull the bike up and put it back down to earth, this is how the best downhill racers deal with rocks, etc. They also use rocks as jumps or launch ramps to fly over the remainder of the rocky section. It's rather like watching ballet or gymnastics, where the bike and rider skip from one smooth rock to the next. Pump the suspension, using momentum and gravity to keep the flow of speed enough to ride out the section.

" use the terrain to your advantage "

Pre-jumping

At world-class level, racers use the pre-jump technique to jump into bomb-holes or steep drops, landing on the near vertical face to get a smoother line. This also means they have jumped over the lip that develops at the top of such drops and can often send you launching into space. By pre-jumping the lip, the rider is more in control, not being at the command of the terrain. It is also faster to stay closer to the ground for the main, as being miles in the air opens up more opportunity for big crashes. And we have the scars to prove it. Pre-jumping is about being a few inches off the ground and is a form of 'ironing out' the lumps and bumps that slow you down or, worse still, have you off. It's possible to use pre-jumping to jump ditches and

hollows too, so don't limit the technique to obstacles that stick up on the track. It's a valuable skill and can get you out of loads of trouble when you're going fast. If pre-jumping is totally new to you then start with just getting the front wheel over, more often than not the back end will just follow and is capable of looking after itself at speed.

So, don't waste time gawping at the surrounding scenery, focus on where you're going and get on with it. If you know the track, practice sections to perfect the best and fastest line for you and then put it all together for the smoothest run. If you're dead serious about making it to the bottom first, try using a stopwatch like the best downhillers use on their racecourse practice runs. By comparing times, this method allows you to gauge how you are improving.

Opposite: "Use rocks and bumps as launch ramps for pre-jumping hollows or obstacles."

Right: "Look beyond your front wheel to the world ahead." – Steve. The White Church, Lefkas, Greece.

9
catching air

Jumping. We've all tried it, and with varying degrees of success. Admit it – at some time or another, the majority of us have made ramps out of bits of wood and a brick or two in the street. Maybe the jumping we do out in the woods today has really changed very little since the days when, as a kid, Evel Knievel was our sole inspiration. Either way, it's a similar jump principle – you go up and then you come back down.

If only it *were* that simple. What's more annoying when you're just starting out on a career in the air is that the professional riders really do make it look that simple, and to top it off they stick a trick or two in there whilst they're doing it. Just bear in

mind that they all started off small, and then progressed to the bigger stuff to get to where they are today.

Jumping off smaller ledges or rocks is an excellent way of getting to grips with the 'time in the air feeling'. It gives your stomach a good chance to get used to what it feels like once the upward momentum ceases and things start to fall... literally. A good take-off is essential, just riding up to a drop and letting the front fall away will only end in tears as you watch your front wheel plummet to the ground with you closely following behind. As you approach the lip, pull up on the bars by pushing your body weight backwards. Exaggerate it and really try to keep the front wheel up or horizontal with the rear wheel, that way you'll be in control as you enter the air. Landing takes a bit of thought too; unfortunately it's all too easy to allow the bike to slam into the ground. If you let both wheels hit at the same time it's a pretty safe bet you'll be okay. But to land in a fashion that allows you to roll out of the landing without jolting or stopping when the wheels touch down is the ultimate goal. Absorbing the shock with your arms and legs allows you to place the bike down gently and decelerate your body. As the bike drops, your limbs will extend or straighten. Use this on landing and bend them to absorb the shock and push the bike forwards to transfer momentum.

Opposite: Keep the front wheel up when dropping off ledges – it will save your face on the landing!

Right: "You can get reasonable height even off small mounds. These are great for beginners." – Steve

Table-tops

Once you are happy landing from the smaller stuff, it's time to head down to the BMX track or dual slalom course and choose a smallish table-top to practice on. A 'table-top' is a jump that has an up-slope (or take-off), then a flat section followed by a down-slope. The idea is that if you can't clear the whole jump from take-off to landing on the down-slope, then you won't suffer too much by coming up short. Table-tops are also a good tool for practising the different elements of a jump, ie the take-off or landing parts. Start by rolling the jump without pedalling too hard. Keep both wheels on the ground as you go and get a feel of the jump's angles. Next, work on the take-off by hitting the jump at a faster, yet still controlled speed and allow the bike to

come up underneath you and (hopefully) leave the ground at the lip of the jump. Remember – start off small. As you progress and gain more air between your wheels and the ground, try to push the bike into the face of the take-off ramp, allowing you to 'pump' into the jump and use the extra energy created to gain more height. Kind of like causing an explosion, but smaller. After a while you may be making some height, but what about clearing the flat section and hitting that down-slope? It's a lot more comfortable to land on a slope.

To get to the down-slope, try pushing the bars forward by straightening your arms and also pushing the bike forwards as you are in the air. Then, as you get closer to the landing ramp, let the front end drop slightly (so that the wheels are roughly at the same angle as the down-slope) and aim to at least get the front wheel on the down-slope. It often helps to look beyond the down-slope, and, surprisingly enough, this method often works, allowing you to land where you looked. If you still can't hit that down-slope then try for more speed and height, that way you'll have more of a chance to reach your target. For more height, allow your body to rise as you take-off, giving your bike a little pull up on the way, then transfer the momentum forwards by pushing the bike and finally angling the nose down to match the slope of the landing ramp.

Opposite: Try pushing the bike forwards when in the air – just push forward on the bars.

Right: "When you're used to being in the air try pulling the bike around and think about some tricks." – Steve

riders' tips

Doubles

Once you've got table-tops dialled, try a small set of doubles (two peak-like jumps one after the other) and use the same techniques and skills – just don't look too hard at the gap in between when you start. It's really a psychological barrier, if you look down into the gap then you could well hit the up-slope of the second jump. And that really stings!

Beyond all the jumping basics that we've just run through, there are a multitude of jumping tricks and stunts to get your head around. They just require enough time in the air to initiate the trick and then have enough time to recover and land the bike.

"If you've only ever ridden a full-suspension bike, now is the time to drag out a hardtail and learn to jump properly from scratch. That way you won't be letting the suspension do the work or get you out of trouble. Learning to ride smoothly and land softly is the key to jumping well and you'll learn that best on a hardtail. It also allows you to hit the jump at a lower speed and still gain height to clear it.

Start by pumping a set of doubles, keeping the wheels on the ground and pushing down on the down-slope of the jump. Try to find a series of doubles or a rhythm section and slightly unweight the pedals on the up-slope of the jump. Keep trying and learn to transfer your body weight to gain speed through the jumps. Learning to pump the bike properly helps with timing, balance and understanding how to keep momentum through jumps, even if you don't want to jump them."
– Steve

Opposite: "I prefer jumping on my hardtail bike, it's easier to throw around." – Steve

"what's keeping you down?"

You can never learn enough about jumping, at the moment I'm riding a fully rigid bike and learning to do a Superman properly. The hardest part is trying to get a complete stretch and push the bike away from the body. It's all about timing really, getting back on is the easy part. I like practising on my rigid bike, it feels more pure – as you hit the jump there's no

suspension compression and the bars are closer to you allowing you to feel exactly how the bike is responding and moving forwards into the air.

If the front end is slightly too high in mid-air, a quick pull of the rear brake will pull the front end down due to gyroscopic effect.

With experience you'll learn exactly which gear you need to clear a certain sized gap and what length run-up and speed you can get away with.

I could go on forever giving tips but you'll only ever get to grips with your jumping by putting in the hours. And probably crashes too.

Left: "Once you've got jumping sussed, get started on the tricks." – Steve

Right: Cliff drops take some building up to – Quarry near Doncaster, Yorkshire.

10
advanced
techniques:
street riding and trials

If the mud and rain put you off riding your regular countryside trails in the winter months, then how about a spot of street riding. Yep, the streets of your home town have more to offer than just high street shops and pedestrians – although these can make for interesting moving slalom poles too. After dark, the deserted streets offer you a good place to perfect riding down steps and jumping off wall jumps.

Check out the library steps or the wall around the bank, or what about the benches in the precinct? Street riding is a form of trials whichever way you look at it. Only to the hardcore off-road riders like us,

it is just another place to ride. However, we wouldn't suggest the steps outside the police station. They may look perfect for practising your pre-jump technique, but sometimes the inhabitants don't appreciate your presence!

Even the simple old kerb is a good place to practice the skills you use on the trials. What's the difference between wheelying up a kerb or the root of an oak tree? Riding along a wall and jumping off the end is the same in principle as holding a line through a tricky section or on the edge of a rut. The theory is the same but where can you go off-road riding with the added benefit of

over-head lights? Nowhere I know, so for the bad weather winter months try exploring the alleyways and streets around town with a group of mates. You'll be pleasantly surprised, the reason that street riding has recently become an underground scene in its own right. It also means you can nip out for a pizza whilst practising. How's that for a perk?

For the real trials gods, the town is heaven with all its buildings, walls, pillars and posts. How some trials riders realise their talent, I don't know, but they must like the pain of trying the almost impossible. To a professional trials rider, jumping off a building and landing lightly onto the rear wheel is a matter-of-course procedure. Unbelievable to most of us is that the wheel doesn't fold in half on impact.

If you fancy attempting something smaller, like a wall for instance, think about pivoting the bike using your arms and legs, a finger over the rear brake lever helps in case you pull the front wheel up too far. It's probably best to be confident with your wheelie technique before going for the real slow and more crucial drops. Unbelievable maybe, but the basic wheelie can open up a whole new dimension to your riding, whatever the terrain.

Staying light and agile on the bike is the key, as well as an incredible natural sense of balance. Practising 'track-stands' (keeping the bike upright whilst motionless with both of your feet on the pedals) is the first step. Learning to stay upright and stable on the spot helps you to understand how any small changes in your weighting or body movements affect the bike.

For the basic track-stand think about balancing the bike using forwards and backwards momentum as well as tilting it from side to side. Turning the front wheel can help but the brakes and pedal pressure are more fundamental. Using your knees against the frame can help with fine balancing once you've got the pedal versus brake theory sussed out.

You'll find muscles you never knew you had the first few times you try. You'll also have bruises you don't remember causing and several you definitely *will* remember how they got there, so wear leg armour and preferably arm protection too. In fact, we can only recommend full body protection at all times or you'll be a mass of scars and bruises. Not that it really matters, because you'll be a far better rider for it and that is, after all, the aim of the game.

Opposite: Wheelying off big drops onto flat concrete takes some guts as well as perfect timing.

Right: Honing those skills you learnt as a kid looks good and helps your other riding too.

11
glossary

Apex: Mid-point of a turn.
Arse over the back: Politely put, putting your body weight over the rear wheel.
Berm: A built-up or banked corner that allows you to maintain speed around a bend.
Bomb-hole: A deep depression in the ground.
Bunny-hop: A technique where the wheels of the bike leave the ground and the bike continues to travel forwards.
Camber: The slope of the ground, 'off-camber' slopes away from the direction in which you are riding.
Cantilever brake: Traditional, short-armed mountain bike brake, cable operated.
Carve: The same as on a snowboard or surfboard when a turn, usually on a berm, is ridden aggressively and smoothly.
Chicken sticks: Slang for brake levers.
Clunker: Early mountain bikes based on Schwinn Beach Cruiser (or similar) bikes.
Coaster brake: Braking mechanism connected to pedal stroke, back-pedalling causes the brake to engage.
Cross-country: The standard type of mountain biking encapsulating all types of riding over distance.
Decreasing/Increasing radius corners: The corner tightens/opens along its length.
DH: Abbreviation for downhill.
Disc brakes: Hub-based discs used instead of rim brakes, as on motorbikes and cars.
Double jump: Two mounds or jumps close enough together to be jumped as one.

Drop-off: A steep bank or slope to be jumped or sometimes ridden down.
Dual slalom: Type of racing where two riders race down the same course over jumps and obstacles.
Flow: When bike and rider move in harmony.
Freeride: An informal, non-competitive form of riding that takes in jumping, downhill and trials.
Full suspension: A bike featuring suspension at the front (forks) and rear part of the frame that holds the back wheel.
Groupset: Group of bicycle components (especially gears/brakes), usually originating form one manufacturer, ie 'Shimano XT'.
Hardtail: A bike featuring a rigid (not full suspension) frame, but featuring suspension forks.
Line: Your chosen riding route, usually through a technical section.
Mafac cantilever brakes: Original cantilever brakes taken from cyclo-cross and touring bikes.
Marin County: Wilderness area north of San Francisco, California, USA.
MTB: Abbreviation of mountain bike.
Nicolas Vouilloz: French rider who is seven times UCI Downhill World Champion.
Pre-jumping: Technique to jump before an obstacle to smooth out terrain.
Pulling up: Lifting the front wheel off the ground by pulling at the bars.

Pumping: Pushing the bike through difficult terrain or bumps, forcing the wheels along the ground and weighting the bike to induce momentum.

Raggedy: When your riding style goes to pot due to excess speed.

Railed: A corner ridden at full speed, almost at the limit.

Reference points: A memorable point on the trails used as a reminder to turn, brake or pedal, etc.

Repack Races: Series of downhill races in Marin County, California, during the seventies.

Roadie: Someone who rides a road bike and/or on the road, someone who has not 'seen the light'!

Set-up: The way in which a bike is built and adjusted to suit the rider.

Shimano: Leading Japanese component manufacturer.

Singletrack: Narrow track wide enough for one rider, usually through woodland or on steep slopes.

Sketchy: Those slightly out of control moments that may, or may not be rectifiable.

Skid: A product of harsh braking where the wheel locks and the tyre loses traction with the ground.

Stack: A crash, usually unpleasant.

Staying fluid: Keeping momentum going and using speed to overcome obstacles.

Stiffback: See 'Roadie'.

Street riding: Riding in towns using man-made structures as obstacles.

Superman: A mid-air trick emulating that old time favourite Superman's flight technique, only with a bike.

Table-top jump: A mound with a flat surface on top, the slopes either side are used to take-off and land on when jumping.

Technical: As in 'technical section', a part of the trail that is strewn with rocks, roots or tight turns to test the rider's skill.

Technique: Skills or a series of skills used to ride a bike.

Track-stand: A technique where bike and rider are balanced on the spot using brakes and pedals to maintain balance.

Traction: The grip of the tyres on the ground.

Trails: Tracks or paths for riding along, varying in technical difficulty depending on terrain.

Trials riding: Extreme riding over large, sometimes man-made obstacles such as barrels and cars.

V-brake: Linear pull, long-armed, cable-operated cantilever brake.

Weighting/unweighting: Moving of body weight on different parts of the bike, such as pedals or bars.

Wheelie: A technique where the front wheel is lifted off the ground and the bike is ridden on the rear wheel.

XC: Abbreviation for cross-country.

Chilli is the global agency specialising in Freesports such as mountain biking.

Chilli provides services and products which include strategic consultancy, campaign implementation, event and TV production, media exploitation and design.

To find out more about the range of Freesports video titles available from Chilli visit chillivideo.com

For more information on Chilli please contact: info@chilli-news.com

Other titles available in this series:

The Ultimate Guide to Windsurfing
The Ultimate Guide to Surfing

Forthcoming titles from Chilli and HarperCollins*Publishers*:

The Ultimate Guide to Snowboarding
The Ultimate Guide to Skateboarding
The Ultimate Guide to In-line Skating